Celebrate
the
50 States!

written and illustrated by **Loreen Leedy**

Holiday House
New York

This book is dedicated to the men and women who founded our nation.

Key to Labels

State rank	22nd
Year entered Union	1819
State capital	*Montgomery*
Town	*Huntsville*
State bird and flower	Yellowhammer, Camellia
Other animal	Opossum
Place or event	*Tuskegee Institute*
Product from state	paper pulp
Scale of map	*60 miles*
Ocean or Lake	*Gulf of Mexico*
River	*Chattahoochee River*

Copyright © 1999 by Loreen Leedy
All rights reserved
Printed in the United States of America

Library of Congress Cataloging-in-Publication Data
 Leedy, Loreen.
Celebrate the 50 states / written and illustrated by Loreen Leedy.
p. cm.
Summary: Introduces statistics, emblems, notable cities, products, and other facts about the fifty states, United States territories, and Washington, D.C.
ISBN 0-8234-1431-0
1. U.S. states Miscellanea Juvenile literature. 2. United States Miscellanea Juvenile literature. [1. United States Miscellanea.]
I. Title.
E180.L44 1999   973—dc21   99-10986   CIP
ISBN 0-8234-1631-3 (pbk.)

Thanks to my brother Robert Leedy for his help in finding reference materials.

Clayton

Here is what you'll find in this book:

Arizona

Arizona has a dry climate and unusual scenery, with mesas, canyons, and rock formations.

48th
1912

100 miles

The Grand Canyon

Monument Valley

Petrified Forest National Park

Flagstaff•

The Arizona Meteor Crater

Irrigation helps us grow.

The Petrified Forest is full of fossilized trees.

Phoenix

Tucson•

OK CORRAL

Cactus Wren

Saguaro Cactus Flower

How deep and how long is the Grand Canyon?

Navajo weavers make beautiful wool rugs.

Arkansas

Arkansas is called the natural state, because of its mountains, forests, waterfalls, lakes, rivers, and mineral springs.

25th
1836

Fayetteville•

Ozark Folk Center

Bobcat

Little Rock

Rice Fields

Hot Springs•

Mississippi River

60 miles

RICE

Turkey Tidbits

Mockingbird

You may have eaten rice and processed foods from this state.

What precious stones can be dug up in Arkansas?

Apple Blossom

We like to go canoeing on the Buffalo River.

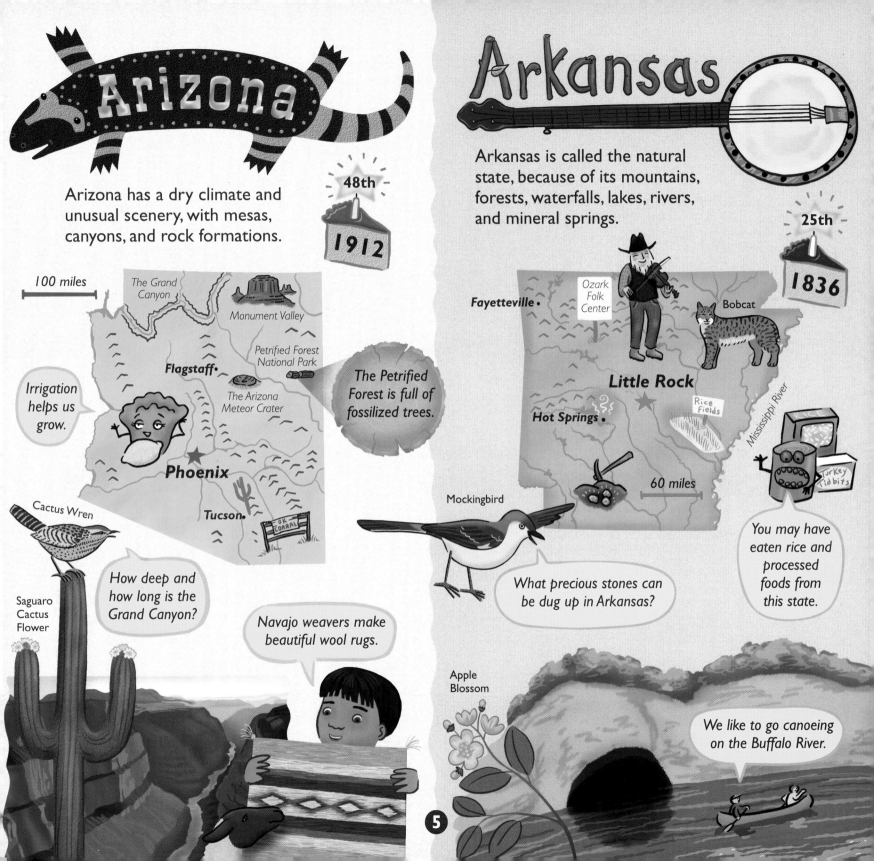

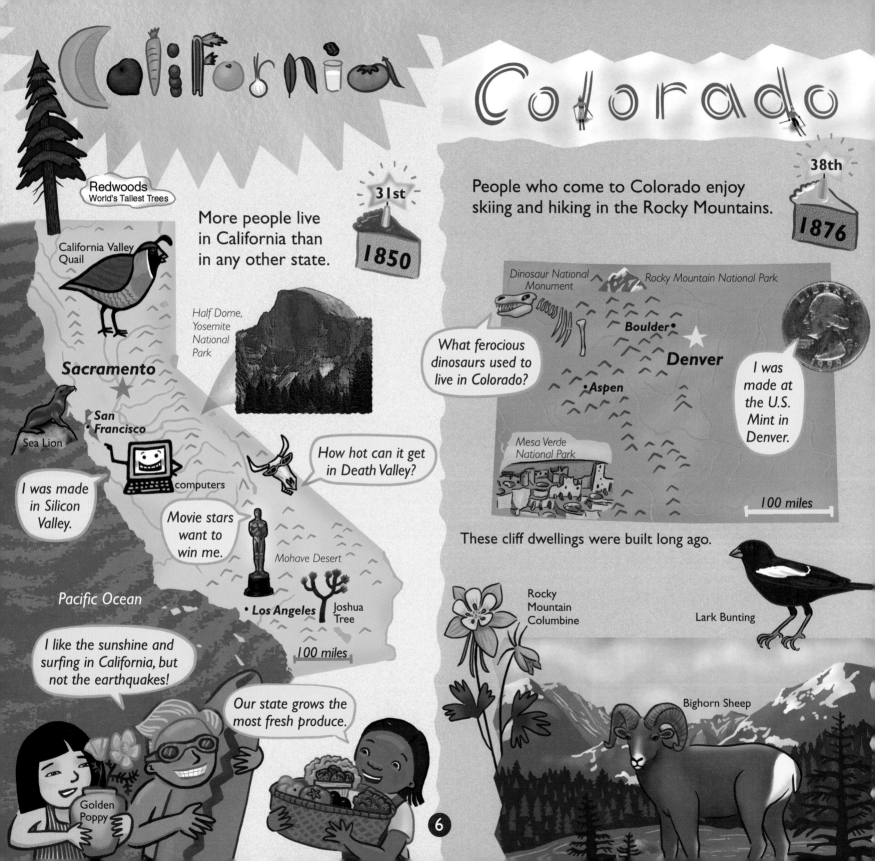

CONNECTICUT

5th
1788

Robin

Connecticut's factories make submarines, clocks, helicopters, hardware, locks, and silverware.

clocks

30 miles

Hartford

Mountain Laurel

Raccoon

Who wrote America's first dictionary?

YALE

New Haven

Mystic

Long Island Sound

submarines

Mystic Seaport is a restored 19th-century waterfront town.

Delaware

1st
1787

Delaware was the first of the 13 colonies to become a state.

What was invented here in 1935?

Wilmington

Blue Hen Chicken

Bombay Hook Wildlife Refuge

Dover

Delaware Bay

I hatched in southern Delaware.

chickens

Rehoboth Beach

Atlantic Ocean

30 miles

We go to Rehoboth Beach for vacation!

Peach Blossom

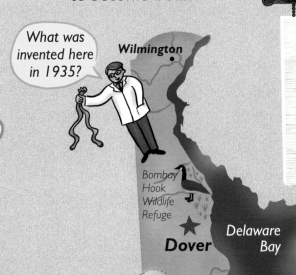

Florida

27th
1845

Florida is a flat peninsula with more than a thousand miles of sandy beaches.

What is the largest wetlands on earth?

Mockingbird

Gulf of Mexico

Manatee

100 miles

Theme Parks!

Orlando

Tallahassee

Kennedy Space Center

grapefruit

FLORIDA

Orange Blossom

honey

Bottle-nosed dolphin

Miami

The Everglades

Florida Keys

Alligator

Atlantic Ocean

Cherokee Rose

watermelon

peanuts   peaches

Georgia

4th
1788

Georgia is the largest state east of the Mississippi River.

One end of the Appalachian Trail is in Georgia. How far does it go?

Stone Mountain

Atlanta

pecans

Grown in Georgia

Masters Golf Tournament

Augusta

Brown Thrasher

80 miles

Savannah

Okefenokee Swamp

Cypress Tree

Atlantic Ocean

Civil rights leader Martin Luther King, Jr., was born in Atlanta.

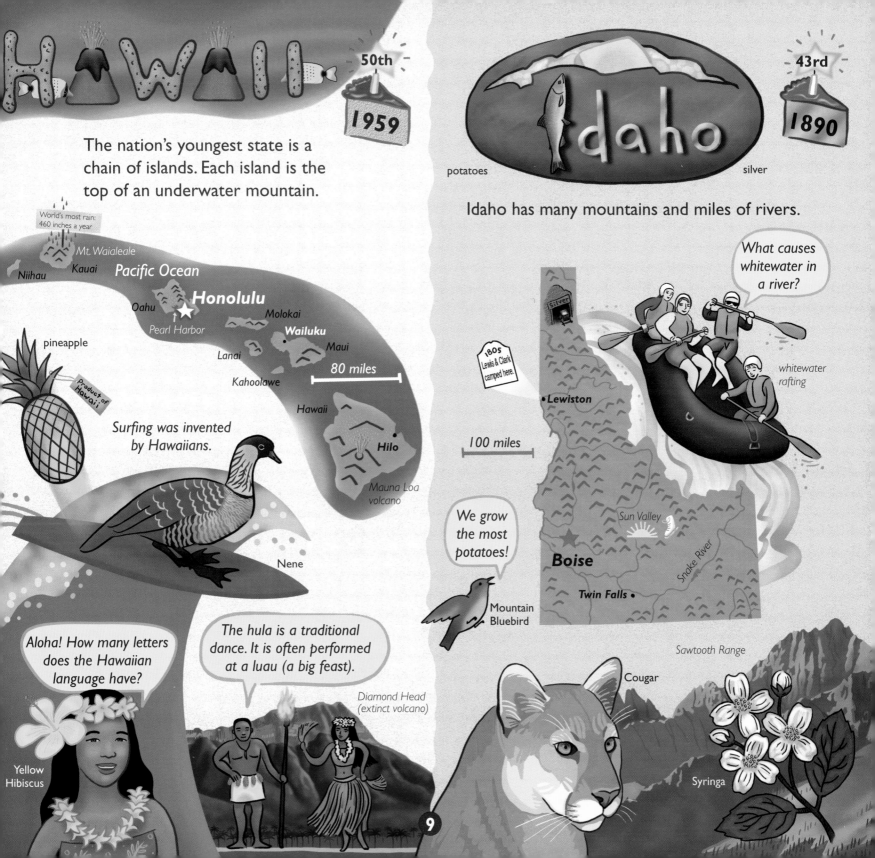

HAWAII

50th
1959

The nation's youngest state is a chain of islands. Each island is the top of an underwater mountain.

World's most rain: 460 inches a year

Mt. Waialeale

Niihau Kauai **Pacific Ocean**

Oahu **Honolulu** Molokai

Pearl Harbor **Wailuku**

pineapple Lanai Maui

Product of Hawaii Kahoolawe 80 miles

Hawaii

Surfing was invented by Hawaiians.

Hilo

Mauna Loa volcano

Nene

Aloha! How many letters does the Hawaiian language have?

The hula is a traditional dance. It is often performed at a luau (a big feast).

Diamond Head (extinct volcano)

Yellow Hibiscus

idaho

43rd
1890

potatoes silver

Idaho has many mountains and miles of rivers.

What causes whitewater in a river?

Silver

1805 Lewis & Clark camped here.

whitewater rafting

100 miles

• Lewiston

We grow the most potatoes!

Sun Valley

Boise

Snake River

Twin Falls •

Mountain Bluebird

Sawtooth Range

Cougar

Syringa

ILLINOIS

railroad cars

21st
1818

Indiana

19th
1816

Illinois has quiet farms in the countryside and busy urban areas. Chicago is a great city that is a hub for shipping by land, air, and water.

How many stories does the Sears Tower have?

Illinois Violet

Lake Michigan

Chicago

• **Peoria**

Springfield

soybeans

80 miles

The nation's oldest zoo has free admission.

Like other Midwestern states, Indiana has cornfields, small towns, cold winters, and hot summers.

Lake Michigan

80 miles

• **Gary**

Peony

Ft. Wayne •

Children's Museum

Cardinal

"Indy 500" Motor Speedway

Indianapolis

Cardinal

Basketball is very popular in Indiana.

Lincoln Boyhood National Memorial

1858
"As I would not be a slave, so I would not be a master."
Abraham Lincoln

Lincoln Park Zoo, Chicago

Abraham Lincoln lived in both Illinois and Indiana. He became one of the country's most beloved presidents.

What is a Hoosier?

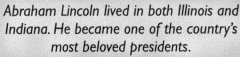

Iowa

hogs

29th
1846

Iowa has over 100,000 farms. The biggest crops are corn and soybeans.

Who painted us?

80 miles

This state has great topsoil!

• Sioux City

Des Moines

• Cedar Rapids

Mississippi River

National Balloon Museum

Wild Rose

My calf won a prize at the Iowa State Fair.

Eastern Goldfinch

CORNDOGS

⑪

Kansas

34th
1861

The flat plains of Kansas grow wheat and other "amber waves of grain." Many private airplanes and small jets are made in Wichita.

◎ Geographic Center of the Lower 48 states

Topeka

Why did cowboys come to Dodge City in the 1880s?

World's Largest Salt Deposit

National Teachers Hall of Fame

• Dodge City

• Wichita

100 miles

1932
First Woman to Fly Atlantic Solo
Amelia Earhart was born in Kansas.

helium

Sunflower

Western Meadowlark

Flour

Some foods made of wheat

Kentucky

15th
1792

The Bluegrass State was nicknamed for its blue-green grass.

Kentucky Derby

Kentucky Cardinal

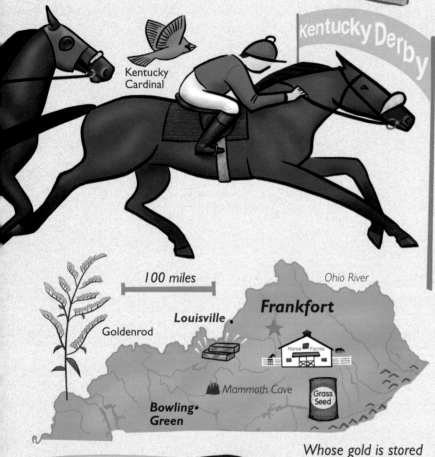

100 miles

Goldenrod

Louisville

Frankfort

Ohio River

Horse Farms

Mammoth Cave

Grass Seed

Bowling Green

Whose gold is stored in Fort Knox?

Mammoth Cave is the largest cave system in the world. It has over 300 miles of passages.

LOUISIANA

18th
1812

The Mississippi River makes New Orleans one of the busiest ports in America.

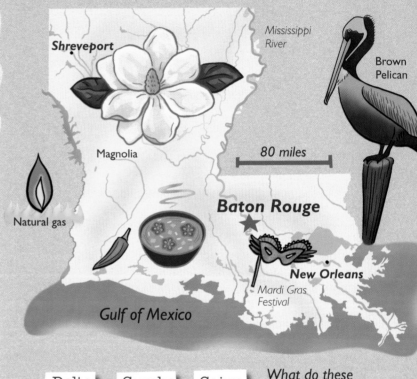

Shreveport

Mississippi River

Magnolia

Natural gas

80 miles

Brown Pelican

Baton Rouge

New Orleans

Mardi Gras Festival

Gulf of Mexico

Delta   Gumbo   Cajun

What do these Louisiana words mean?

Jazz began in New Orleans.

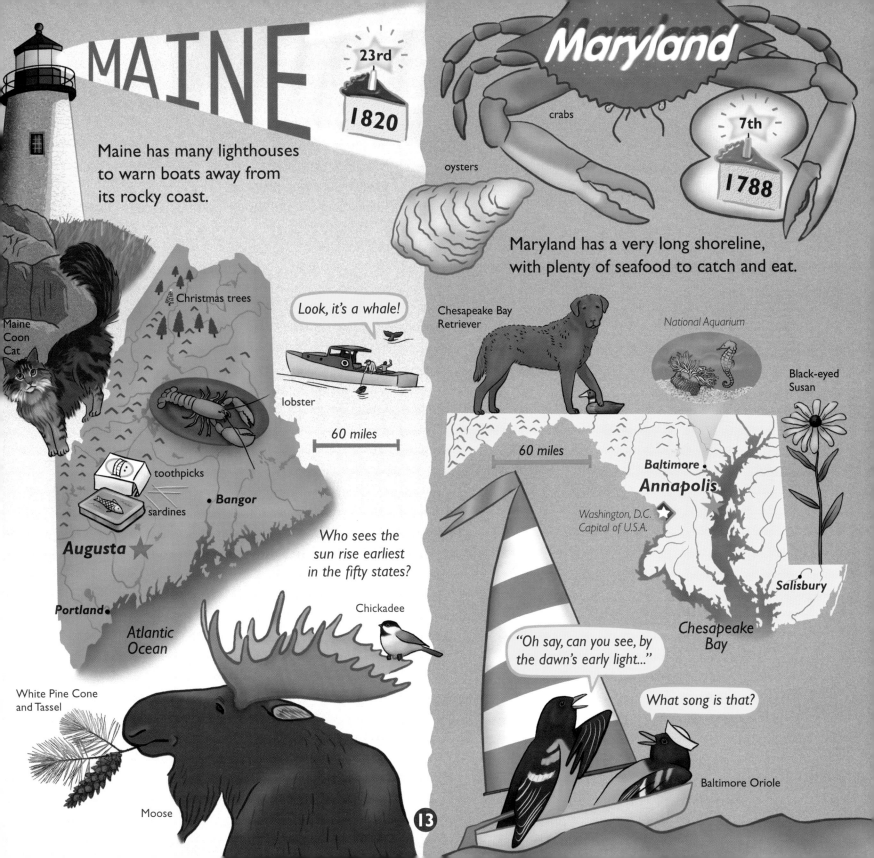

MAINE

23rd
1820

Maine has many lighthouses to warn boats away from its rocky coast.

Christmas trees

Maine Coon Cat

"Look, it's a whale!"

lobster

60 miles

toothpicks

sardines

• Bangor

Augusta

Who sees the sun rise earliest in the fifty states?

Portland•

Atlantic Ocean

Chickadee

White Pine Cone and Tassel

Moose

Maryland

crabs

7th
1788

oysters

Maryland has a very long shoreline, with plenty of seafood to catch and eat.

Chesapeake Bay Retriever

National Aquarium

Black-eyed Susan

60 miles

Baltimore •
Annapolis

Washington, D.C. Capital of U.S.A.

Salisbury•

Chesapeake Bay

"Oh say, can you see, by the dawn's early light..."

What song is that?

Baltimore Oriole

Massachusetts

6th
1788

Many historic events took place in Massachusetts.

Chickadee

1620
Pilgrims land

1621
The First Thanksgiving

1773
The Boston Tea Party

1775
Paul Revere's ride

1636
1st U.S. College
Harvard

SALEM

Cranberries

Worcester •

Boston

Atlantic Ocean

Plymouth •

Cape Cod

40 miles

Mayflower

Cape Cod

What was the name of the Pilgrims' ship?

Codfish

Michigan

26th
1837

Michigan is made of two peninsulas surrounded by four of the Great Lakes.

Apple Blossom

100 miles

Lake Superior

snowmobiling

Mackinac Bridge

Robin

Whitetail Deer

Sleeping Bear Dunes National Lakeshore

Lake Huron

Grand Rapids •

Lansing

Lake Michigan

Flakies! cereal

Detroit •

Lake Erie

What is the nickname for the Lower Peninsula?

Detroit is known as the Motor City because so many cars and trucks are made there.

Minnesota

St. Paul
Winter Carnival

32nd

1858

Minnesota has cold winter weather and many lakes and forests.

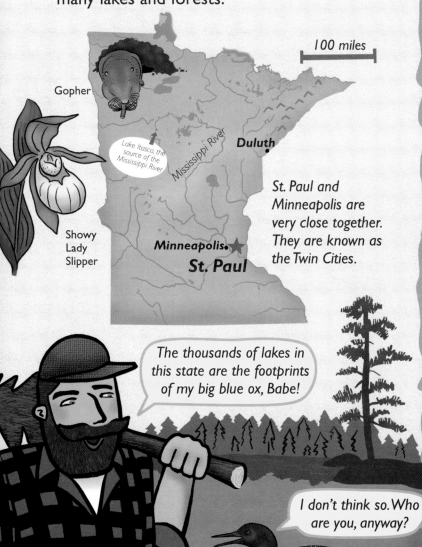

100 miles

Gopher

Lake Itasca, the source of the Mississippi River

Mississippi River

Duluth

Showy Lady Slipper

Minneapolis.
★ **St. Paul**

St. Paul and Minneapolis are very close together. They are known as the Twin Cities.

The thousands of lakes in this state are the footprints of my big blue ox, Babe!

I don't think so. Who are you, anyway?

Loon

15

Mississippi

20th

1817

Mississippi has the look of the Old South, with many pre-Civil War houses still standing.

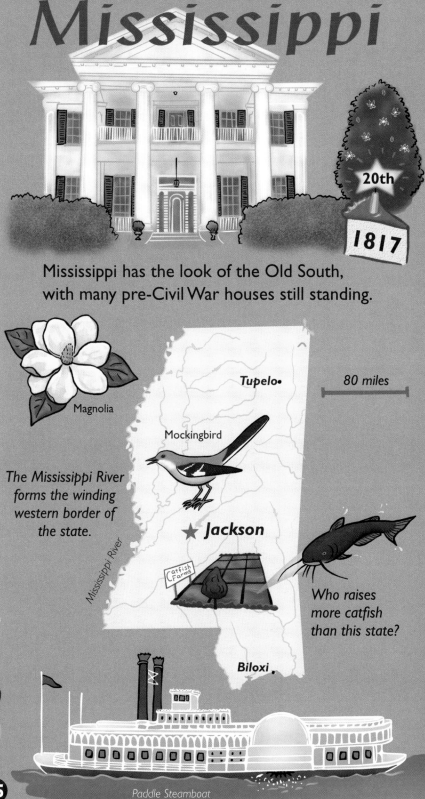

Magnolia

Tupelo•

80 miles

Mockingbird

The Mississippi River forms the winding western border of the state.

Mississippi River

★ **Jackson**

Catfish Farms

Who raises more catfish than this state?

Biloxi.

Paddle Steamboat

Missouri

Missouri was the "Gateway to the West" when many pioneers traveled through.

For how long did the Pony Express deliver mail?

Bluebird

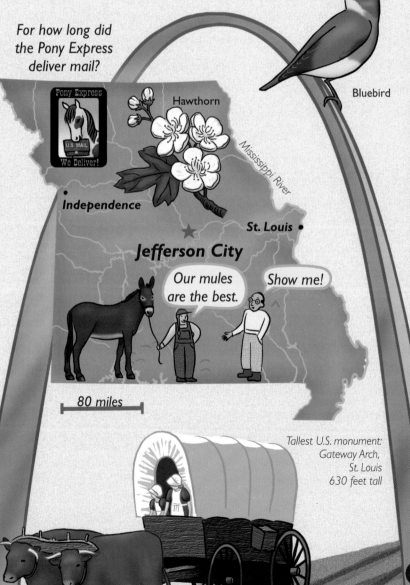

Pony Express
U.S. MAIL
We Deliver!

Hawthorn

Mississippi River

Independence

St. Louis

Jefferson City

Our mules are the best.

Show me!

80 miles

Tallest U.S. monument: Gateway Arch, St. Louis 630 feet tall

Montana

Montana has wide open spaces with fewer than a million residents.

Western Meadowlark

"Big Sky Country" is the state's nickname.

Museum of the Plains Indians

Bitterroot

Missoula

Helena

Billings

150 miles

What are glaciers made of?

Glacier National Park

Mountain Goat

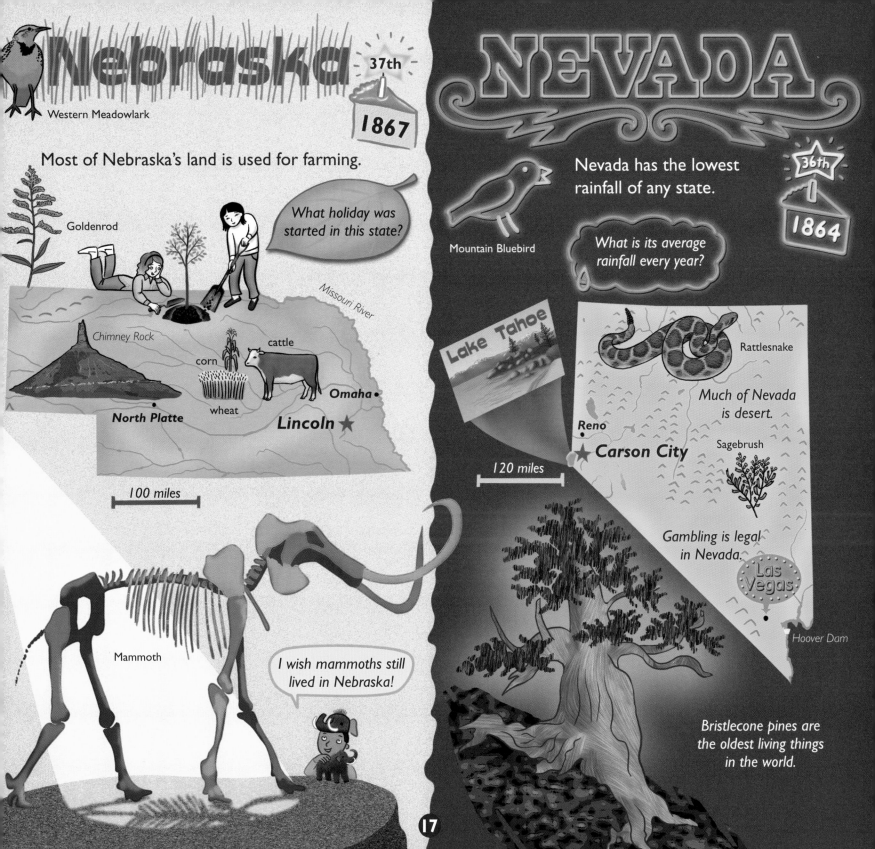

Nebraska

37th
1867

Western Meadowlark

Most of Nebraska's land is used for farming.

Goldenrod

What holiday was started in this state?

Missouri River

Chimney Rock

corn

cattle

wheat

North Platte

Omaha

Lincoln

100 miles

Mammoth

I wish mammoths still lived in Nebraska!

NEVADA

36th
1864

Mountain Bluebird

Nevada has the lowest rainfall of any state.

What is its average rainfall every year?

Lake Tahoe

Rattlesnake

Much of Nevada is desert.

Reno

Carson City

Sagebrush

120 miles

Gambling is legal in Nevada.

Las Vegas

Hoover Dam

Bristlecone pines are the oldest living things in the world.

New Hampshire

9th
1788

New Hampshire's colorful fall leaves, crisp winters, and quiet villages are typical of New England states.

That covered bridge is really long.

Why do they cover bridges, anyway?

Purple Lilac

40 miles

1934
World's fastest wind speed was recorded on Mt. Washington: 231 miles per hour!

Concord

• Manchester

Nashua •

Purple Finch

This state holds the first primary for every presidential election.

VOTE

I am the Old Man of the Mountain.

18

New Jersey

Boardwalk Boogie

New Jersey is densely populated and has many farms and beaches.

3rd
1787

Eastern Goldfinch

Who invented the light bulb in his lab in New Jersey?

Newark •

30 miles

Trenton

Atlantic Ocean

Grown in the Garden State

Cape May has many Victorian-style buildings.

Atlantic City •

Cape May

Purple Violet

New Mexico

Old traditions as well as modern technology are a part of life in New Mexico.

47th

1912

People can build with adobe in a dry climate.

What is adobe?

Pueblo village

Santa Fe

I am a storyteller doll.

• **Albuquerque**

1945
The first atomic bomb tested

Bat

Las Cruces.

Carlsbad Caverns

100 miles

Yucca

Pueblo pottery

Roadrunner

White Sands National Monument

19

NEW YORK

11th

1788

Nature lovers enjoy visiting New York state's mountains and lake shorelines.

Bluebird

100 miles

Lake Ontario

The Finger Lakes are long and thin... like fingers!

Niagara Falls

• **Buffalo**

Albany

New York City is the nation's largest city, with endless things to see and do.

theater

Long Island

art

New York City

finance

shopping

fashion

Statue of Liberty

Rose

New York City skyline

What country gave me to the United States?

North Carolina

North Carolina has mountains in the west, hills in the center, and beaches in the east.

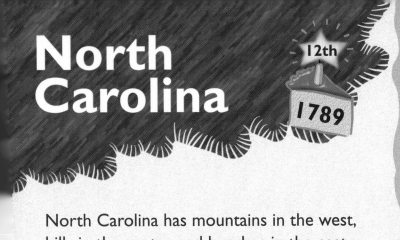

Cardinal

Who made the first airplane flight in 1903?

furniture

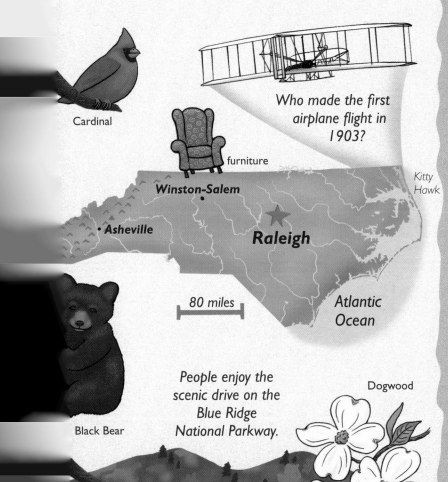

Winston-Salem

Kitty Hawk

Asheville

Raleigh

80 miles

Atlantic Ocean

Black Bear

People enjoy the scenic drive on the Blue Ridge National Parkway.

Dogwood

North Dakota

Homesteaders came to North Dakota in the late 1800s to farm.

WHEAT

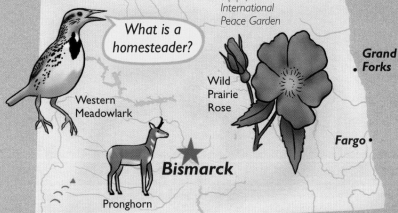

International Peace Garden

What is a homesteader?

Western Meadowlark

Grand Forks

Wild Prairie Rose

Bismarck

Fargo

Pronghorn

100 miles

Theodore Roosevelt National Park

Sitting Bull was a leader of the Sioux Nation.

Ohio

17th
1803

Ohio has many factories that produce rubber, office machines, refrigerators, glass, and more.

Cardinal

Scarlet Carnation

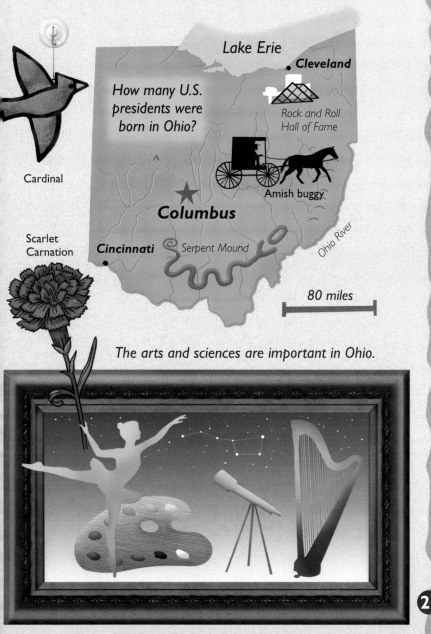

Lake Erie

• Cleveland

Rock and Roll Hall of Fame

How many U.S. presidents were born in Ohio?

Amish buggy

Columbus

Cincinnati

Serpent Mound

Ohio River

80 miles

The arts and sciences are important in Ohio.

Oklahoma

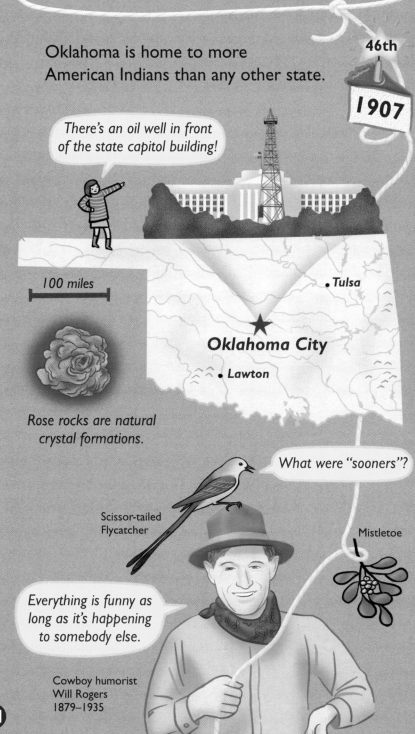

Oklahoma is home to more American Indians than any other state.

46th
1907

There's an oil well in front of the state capitol building!

100 miles

• Tulsa

Oklahoma City

• Lawton

Rose rocks are natural crystal formations.

What were "sooners"?

Scissor-tailed Flycatcher

Mistletoe

Everything is funny as long as it's happening to somebody else.

Cowboy humorist Will Rogers 1879–1935

Oregon

lumber

Western Meadowlark

Immigration to this state began in 1842 along the Oregon Trail.

33rd

1859

100 miles

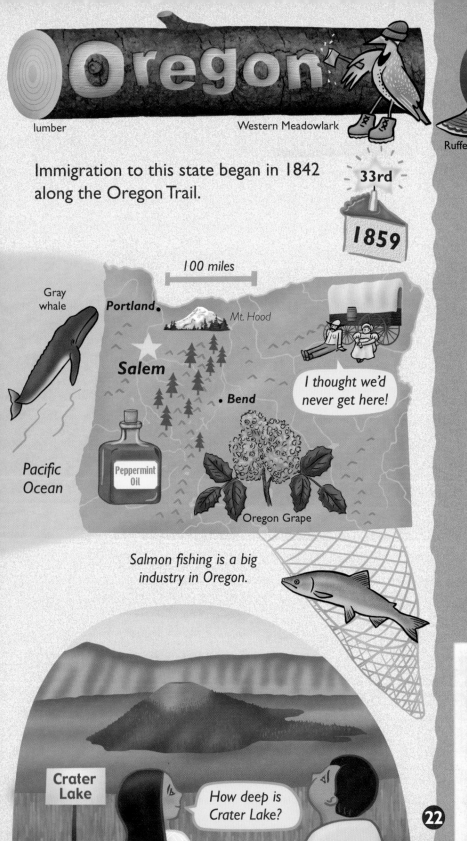

Gray whale

Portland

Mt. Hood

Salem

Bend

I thought we'd never get here!

Pacific Ocean

Peppermint Oil

Oregon Grape

Salmon fishing is a big industry in Oregon.

Crater Lake

How deep is Crater Lake?

Pennsylvania

Ruffed Grouse

In 1776, the Continental Congress signed the Declaration of Independence in Philadelphia.

2nd

1787

60 miles

coal

Mountain Laurel

steel

The Liberty Bell

Harrisburg

Pittsburgh

Philadelphia

Pennsylvania had the nation's first:

library   hospital   art museum   fire department

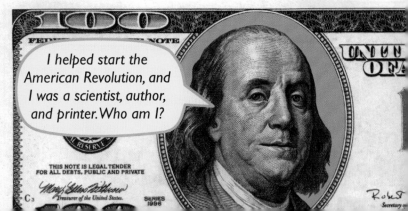

I helped start the American Revolution, and I was a scientist, author, and printer. Who am I?

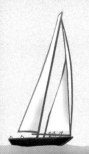

Rhode Island

13th
1790

America's Cup
Yacht Race

Rhode Island is the smallest of the fifty states.

Violet

Is Rhode Island really an island?

Woonsocket

Providence

costume jewelry

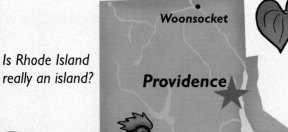
Rhode Island Red

Green Animals Topiary Gardens, Portsmouth

Newport

20 miles

Atlantic Ocean

Rhode Island has many mansions that overlook the ocean.

The Breakers, Newport

23

South Carolina

8th
1788
textiles

South Carolina has hot, humid summers and mild winters.

Yellow jessamine

• Greenville

Carolina Wren

Columbia

peaches

80 miles

sweetgrass basket

Atlantic Ocean

Where did the Civil War begin?

Charleston

Magnolia Gardens, Charleston

Hilton Head lighthouse

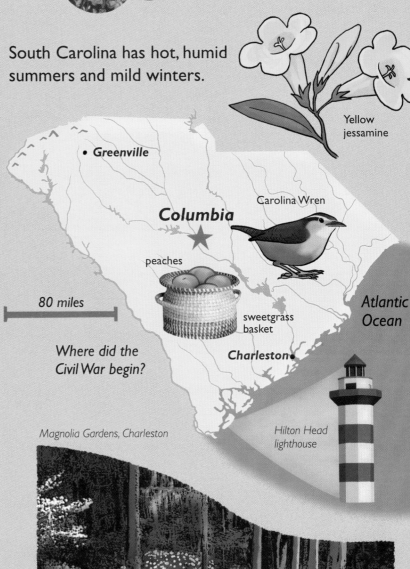

South Dakota

Pasqueflower

Most of South Dakota is prairie grasslands.

Many of my books about pioneer life took place in this state. Who am I?

Ring-necked Pheasant

Pierre

Rapid City

Sioux Falls

Badlands National Park

ring made of Black Hills gold

80 miles

The giant sculpture of four U.S. presidents on Mt. Rushmore is world famous.

Tennessee

Great Smoky Mountains

Tennessee is known for mountains and country music.

Don't be cruel... to a bird so cool...

What famous singer had a mansion in Memphis?

Mockingbird

Mississippi River

Nashville

Knoxville

• **Memphis**

100 miles

hardwood flooring

The steepest passenger railway in the world goes up Lookout Mountain in Chattanooga.

Iris

INCLINE RAILWAY

We can see for miles from up here!

TEXAS

cattle

Texas is a very big state, the second largest.

28th
1845

Just call me Tex.

Bluebonnet

Mockingbird

Dallas

Armadillo

McDonald Observatory

Austin

Houston

mariachi dancers

Gulf of Mexico

oil drilling and refining

180 miles

Why do we "remember the Alamo"?

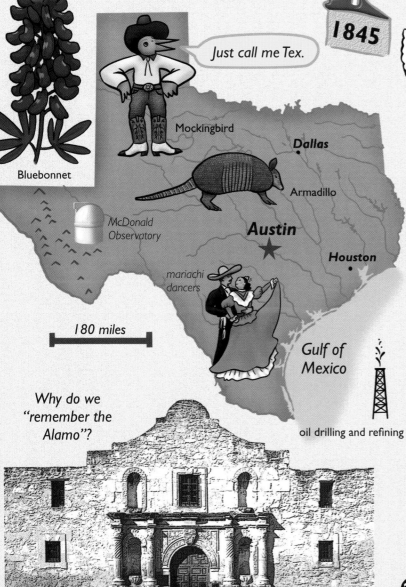

Utah

45th
1896

Petroglyphs

Mormon pioneers came to Utah in 1847.

California Gull

What did seagulls do that helped Utah's settlers to survive?

Great Salt Lake

Ogden

100 miles

Salt Lake City

• **Provo**

copper

snowboarding

Pioneer journal

Bryce Canyon National Park

Arches National Park

Utah's landscape has thousands of fantastic rock formations.

Sego Lily

Vermont

Vermont is a rural state with small towns, villages, and farms.

14th
1791

granite

marble

Red Clover

Green Mountains
• **Burlington**
★ *Montpelier*
• *Rutland*

Hermit Thrush

How do people
make maple syrup?

40 miles

Biking, hiking, and skiing are popular sports in Vermont.

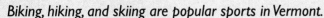

Virginia

The first successful English colony was founded in Jamestown, Virginia, in 1607.

Dogwood

Cardinal

• **Alexandria**

Jamestown artifacts

★ **Richmond**

80 miles

hams

Norfolk •

Atlantic Ocean

Visitors come to Williamsburg to see how the colonists lived.

Candle making

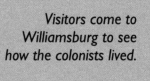

George Washington is known as the father of our country. Why is Virginia nicknamed "Mother of Presidents"?

Washington

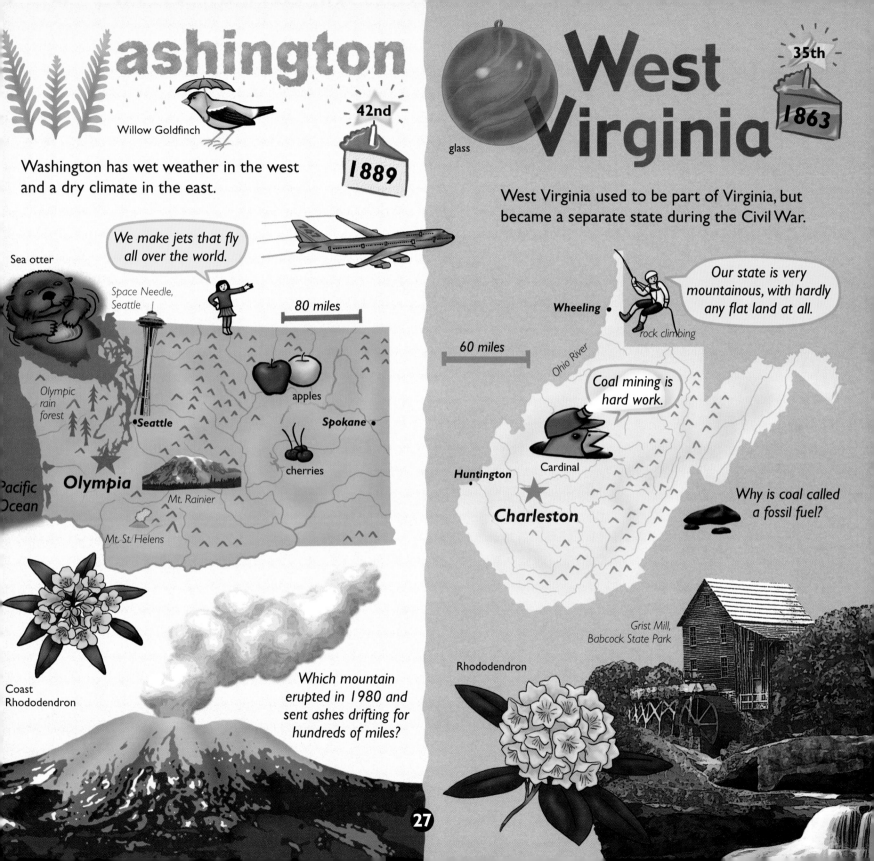

Willow Goldfinch

42nd

1889

Washington has wet weather in the west and a dry climate in the east.

We make jets that fly all over the world.

Sea otter

Space Needle, Seattle

80 miles

Olympic rain forest

apples

•Seattle

Spokane •

Pacific Ocean

Olympia

Mt. Rainier

cherries

Mt. St. Helens

Coast Rhododendron

Which mountain erupted in 1980 and sent ashes drifting for hundreds of miles?

West Virginia

glass

35th

1863

West Virginia used to be part of Virginia, but became a separate state during the Civil War.

Our state is very mountainous, with hardly any flat land at all.

Wheeling •

rock climbing

60 miles

Ohio River

Coal mining is hard work.

Huntington
•

Cardinal

Charleston

Why is coal called a fossil fuel?

Grist Mill, Babcock State Park

Rhododendron

Wisconsin

Badger

1848
cheese

Wisconsin has thousands of lakes that were formed by glaciers a long time ago.

Lake Superior

This state is famous for which group of products?

80 miles

Invented in Wisconsin

Robin

kayaking

Green Bay •

Wood Violet

Lake Michigan

Madison

• **Milwaukee**

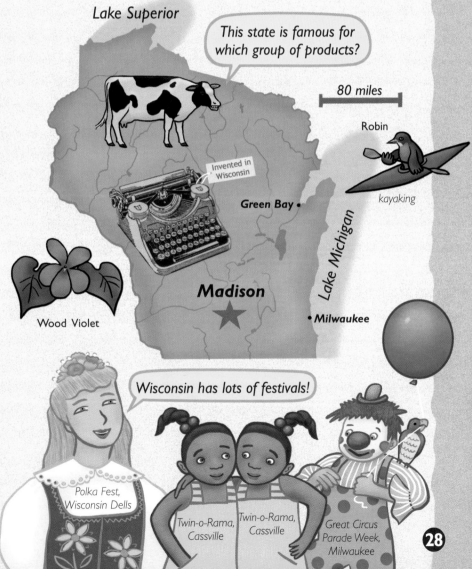
Wisconsin has lots of festivals!

Polka Fest, Wisconsin Dells

Twin-o-Rama, Cassville

Twin-o-Rama, Cassville

Great Circus Parade Week, Milwaukee

Wyoming

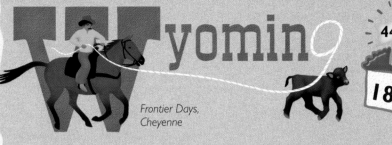
Frontier Days, Cheyenne

1890

Wyoming has the smallest population of all the states.

What was the world's first national park?

Western Meadowlark

Old Faithful Geyser, Yellowstone National Park

Devils Tower

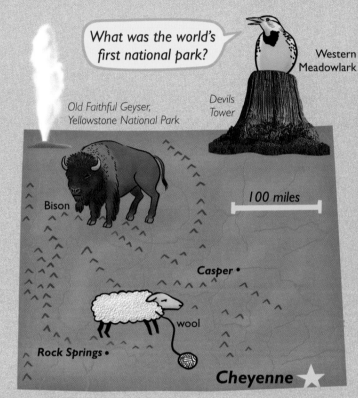
Bison

100 miles

Casper •

wool

Rock Springs •

Cheyenne ⭐

Lower Falls, Yellowstone

Indian Paintbrush

Grizzly bear

28

Washington, D.C.
(District of Columbia)

The U.S. government is located in Washington, D.C. Senators and representatives are elected by each state to come here.

National Zoo

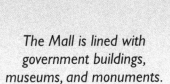
The White House

That's where the president lives!

Which state donated the land where Washington, D.C., now stands?

5 miles

Potomac River

The Mall is lined with government buildings, museums, and monuments.

Lincoln Memorial

Vietnam Veterans Memorial

Washington Monument

Smithsonian Institution

U.S. Capitol

U.S. Territories

The largest U.S. territory is the Commonwealth of Puerto Rico.

Millions of tourists visit the islands every year.

Guam
Agaña

U.S. military bases

40 miles

Guam and American Samoa are small islands in the Pacific.

Pacific Ocean

bananas

San Juan

Puerto Rico

sugar cane

Mayagüez

Ponce

Charlotte Amalie

St. John

St. Thomas

Pago Pago

U.S. Virgin Islands

American Samoa

Atlantic Ocean

Are the people who live in these territories U.S. citizens?

oil refining

St. Croix

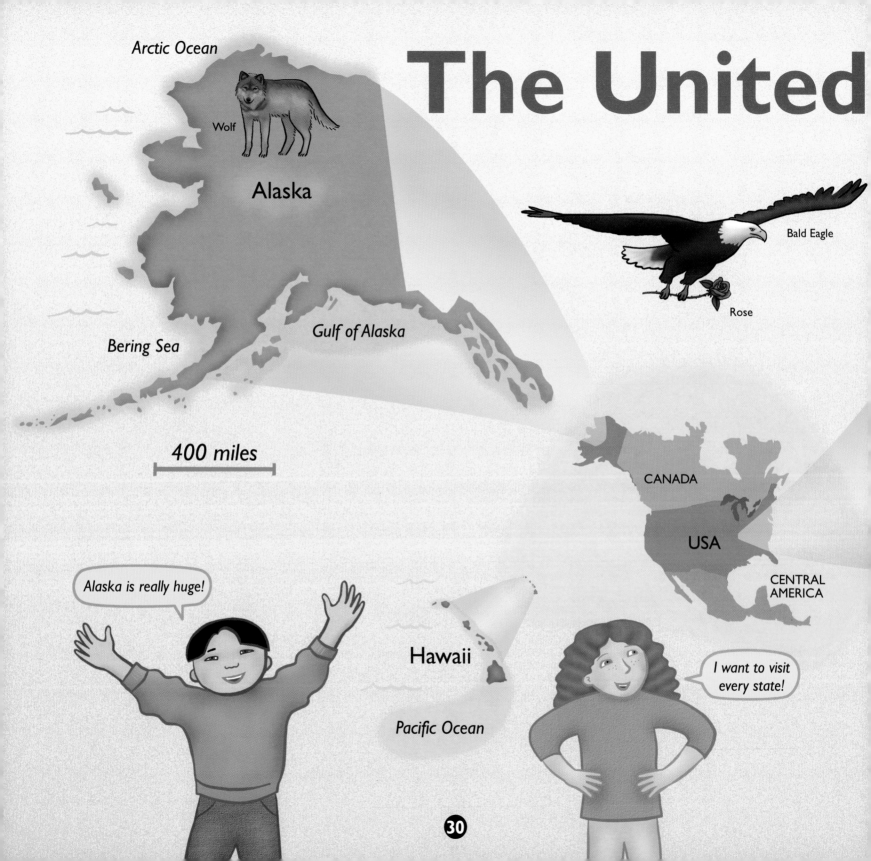

States of America

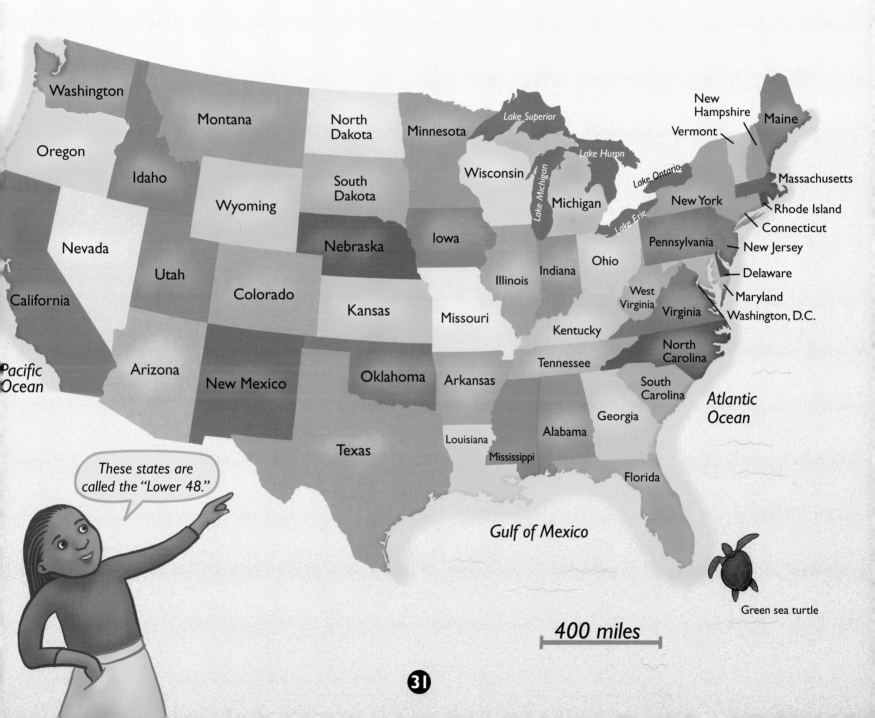

Washington

Oregon

Montana

North Dakota

Minnesota

Lake Superior

New Hampshire

Vermont

Maine

Idaho

Wisconsin

Lake Huron

Lake Ontario

Massachusetts

South Dakota

Michigan

Lake Michigan

Lake Erie

New York

Rhode Island

Wyoming

Connecticut

New Jersey

Nevada

Nebraska

Iowa

Pennsylvania

Delaware

Utah

Ohio

Indiana

West Virginia

Maryland

California

Colorado

Illinois

Virginia

Washington, D.C.

Kansas

Missouri

Kentucky

Pacific Ocean

Arizona

Tennessee

North Carolina

New Mexico

Oklahoma

Arkansas

South Carolina

Atlantic Ocean

Texas

Louisiana

Mississippi

Alabama

Georgia

Florida

These states are called the "Lower 48."

Gulf of Mexico

Green sea turtle

400 miles

Answers

page 4 **AL** In 1955, Rosa Parks refused to give up her bus seat to a white man. Her action led to the Montgomery bus boycott, and eventually to the end of segregation in the South.

AK The U.S. bought Alaska from Russia in 1867 for $7.2 million.

5 **AZ** The Grand Canyon is up to a mile deep and over 200 miles long.

AR Diamonds.

6 **CA** In 1913, the temperature reached 134°F.

CO Tyrannosaurus Rex.

7 **CT** Noah Webster wrote America's first dictionary.

DE Nylon.

8 **FL** The Everglades.

GA The Appalachian Trail runs between Georgia and Maine.

9 **HI** Five vowels (A, E, I, O, U) and seven consonants (H, K, L, M, N, P, W) for a total of twelve letters.

ID Whitewater is caused by water rushing quickly over underwater obstacles, usually rocks.

10 **IL** One hundred and ten stories.

IN "Hoosier" is a nickname for a person from Indiana.

11 **IA** *American Gothic* was painted by Iowa artist Grant Wood.

KS Cowboys used to drive large herds of cattle from Texas to the railroad in Kansas.

12 **KY** The $6 billion worth of gold belongs to the U.S. government.

LA A *delta* is a silt deposit at the mouth of a river. *Gumbo* is a stew made with okra. A *Cajun* is a person of French ancestry.

13 **ME** West Quoddy Head residents are the farthest east.

MD The United States national anthem, *The Star-Spangled Banner*, was written by Maryland native Francis Scott Key.

14 **MA** The Mayflower.

MI The Mitten.

15 **MN** Paul Bunyan, the giant hero of many tall tales.

MS Mississippi is the world's leading producer of pond-raised catfish.

16 **MO** For sixteen months, from April 1860–October 1861.

MT A glacier is a huge sheet of ice and compacted snow.

page 17 **NE** Arbor Day.

NV The average rainfall is about 7 inches a year.

18 **NH** Roofs are put on bridges to save the wood from rotting.

NJ Thomas Edison.

19 **NM** Adobe bricks are made of clay and straw, then dried in the sun.

NY France gave the Statue of Liberty to the U.S. in 1886.

20 **NC** The Wright brothers: Orville flew the airplane while Wilbur ran alongside.

ND A Settler who was given free land (a homestead) if he farmed it.

21 **OH** Seven.

OK The government gave out free land in Oklahoma in 1889. Settlers who claimed land too early were called "sooners."

22 **OR** Crater Lake, about 1,900 feet deep, is the deepest lake in the United States.

PA Benjamin Franklin.

23 **RI** Most of Rhode Island is part of the mainland, though there are several small islands that are part of the state.

SC At Fort Sumter, near Charleston.

24 **SD** Laura Ingalls Wilder wrote *Little House on the Prairie* and other books about her pioneer life.

TN Elvis Presley, who named his mansion Graceland.

25 **TX** Texas volunteers fought a battle against Mexico in 1836, and were trapped in the Alamo.

UT When a swarm of crickets started eating the settlers' crops, a flock of gulls ate the insects.

26 **VT** Sap is drained from maple trees, then boiled into syrup.

VA Eight presidents were born there, including Washington.

27 **WA** Mount St. Helens.

WV Coal is made of fossilized plants that grew millions of years ago. It is burned for fuel or made into chemicals.

28 **WI** Dairy products such as milk and cheese.

WY Yellowstone became the world's first national park in 1872.

29 **DC** Maryland.

Terr. They are U.S. citizens, but can't vote in presidential elections.